HAL•LEONARD® CAJÓN PLAY-ALONG

AUDIO ACCESS INCLUDED

Popular Hits

To access audio visit:
www.halleonard.com/mylibrary

Enter Code
4239-2598-2806-2933

Recording Credits:
Renne Liska: Vocals
Kenny Echizen: Steel String Guitar
Cajón: Ed Roscetti

Produced and Arranged by Ed Roscetti
Cajón Transcriptions by Ed Roscetti
Recorded and Mixed at Roscetti Music, Studio City, CA by Ed Roscetti
Mastered by Andre Mayeux

Ed Roscetti played the Remo Mondo Cajón and the Gon Bops signature Alex Acuna Cajón
with a DW 9000 retrofitted bass drum pedal on this project and used Shure microphones.

Follow Ed Roscetti @roscettimusic on Instagram, Twitter and Facebook.

ISBN 978-1-4803-9312-7

HAL•LEONARD® CORPORATION
7777 W. BLUEMOUND RD. P.O. BOX 13819 MILWAUKEE, WI 53213

Visit Hal Leonard Online at
www.halleonard.com

Brave

Words and Music by Sara Bareilles and Jack Antonoff

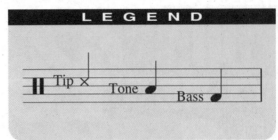

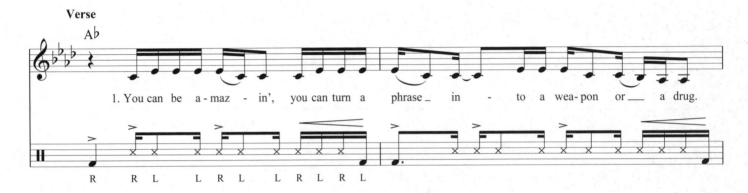

just wan-na see you, _____ just wan-na see you, _____ I wan-na see you be brave. _

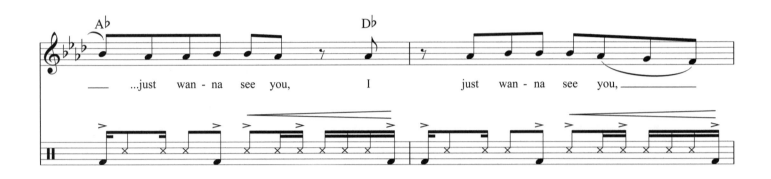

_____ ...just wan-na see you, I just wan-na see you, _____

just wan-na see you, _____ I wan-na see you be brave. ____

Verse

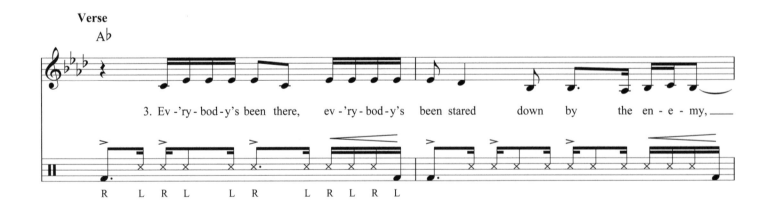

3. Ev-'ry-bod-y's been there, ev-'ry-bod-y's been stared down by the en-e-my, _____

R   L   R   L   L   R   L   R   L   R   L

_____ fall-en for the fear   and   done some dis-ap-pear-in',   bow down   to the might - y. ____

4

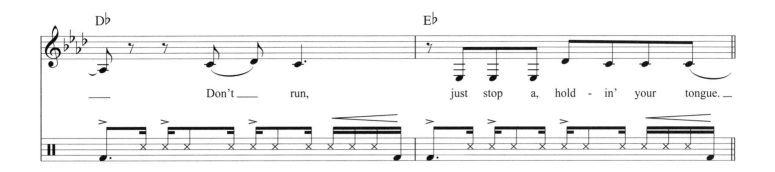

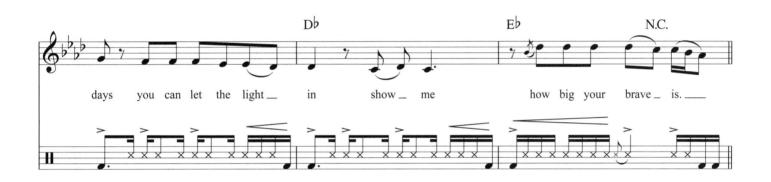

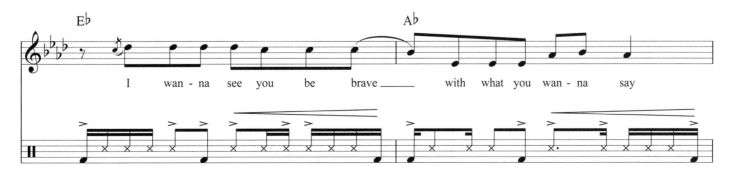

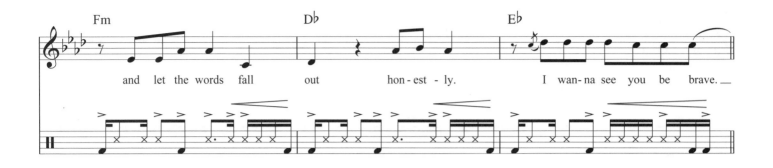

and let the words fall out hon-est-ly. I wan-na see you be brave. ___

Bridge

___ And since your ___ his-to-ry of si-lence won't do you an-y good,

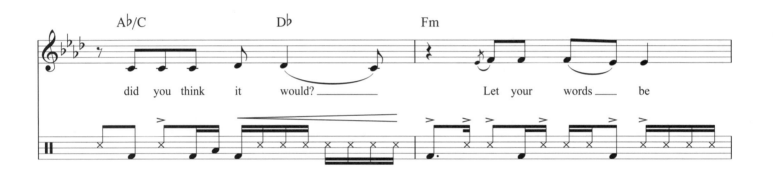

did you think it would? _____ Let your words ___ be

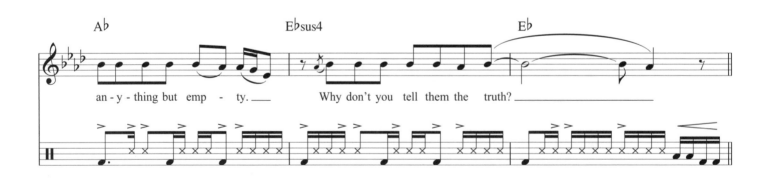

an-y-thing but emp-ty. ___ Why don't you tell them the truth? _____

Chorus

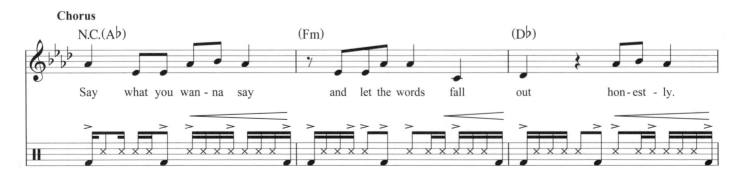

Say what you wan-na say and let the words fall out hon-est-ly.

Outro-Chorus

Bubbly

Words and Music by Colbie Caillat and Jason Reeves

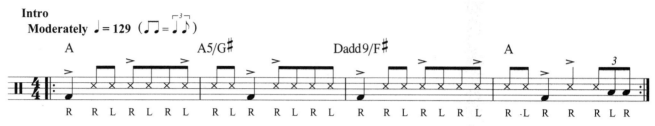

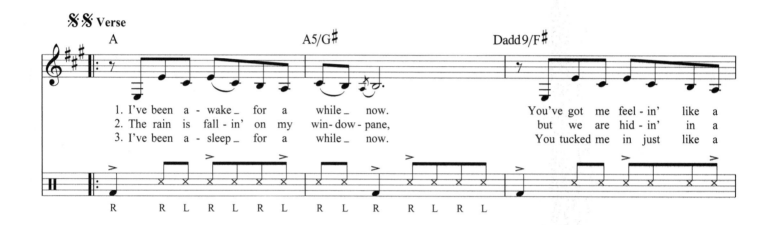

*Played as even eighth notes.

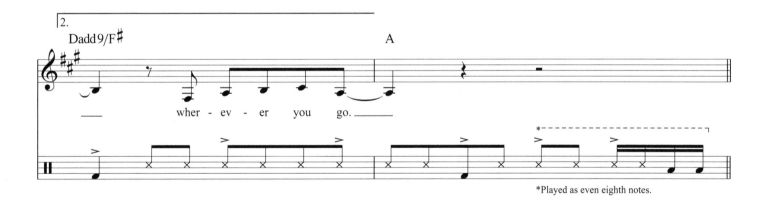

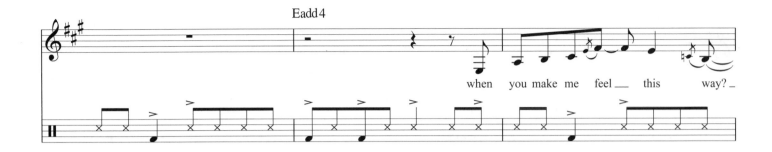

Eadd4

when you make me feel___ this way?___

Bm7   Amaj7/C#

I_____ just..._____

D.S. al Coda 1

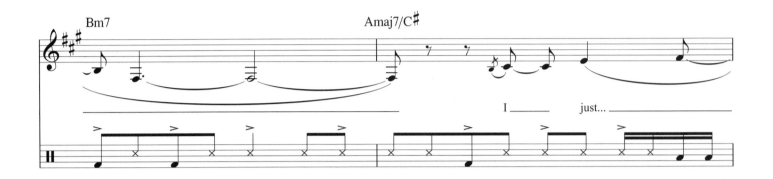

D5

___ Mm._____ And it starts in my toes,___

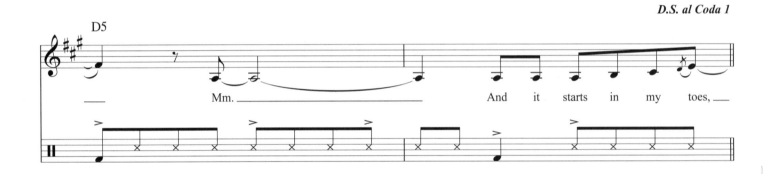

Coda 1

Dadd9/F#   A

___ wher - ev - er you go.___

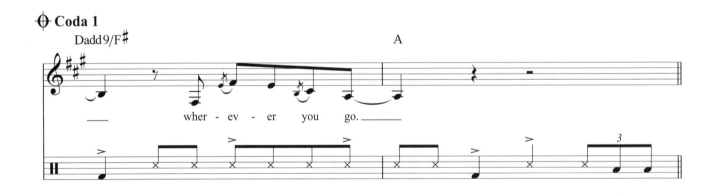

Interlude

A   A5/G#   Dadd9/F#

Da, da, nn, da, da, de, de, de, de, de, de, da, nn, da.

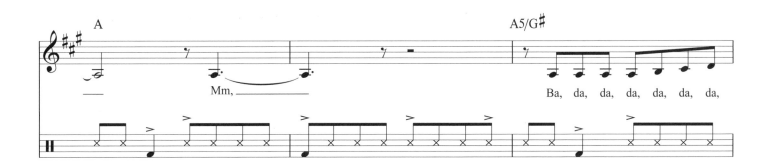

A

A5/G#

Mm, _____

Ba, da, da, da, da, da, da,

D.S.S. al Coda 2

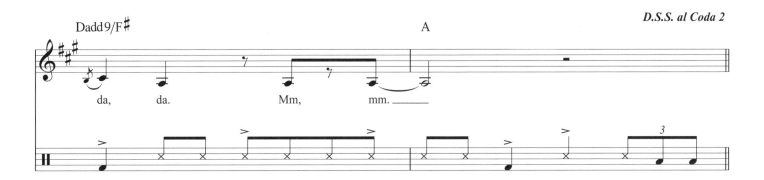

Dadd9/F#

A

da,   da.   Mm,   mm. _____

⊕ Coda 2

End half-time feel

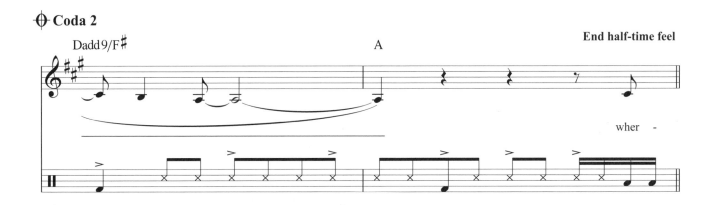

Dadd9/F#

A

wher -

Outro
Slower ♩ = 105

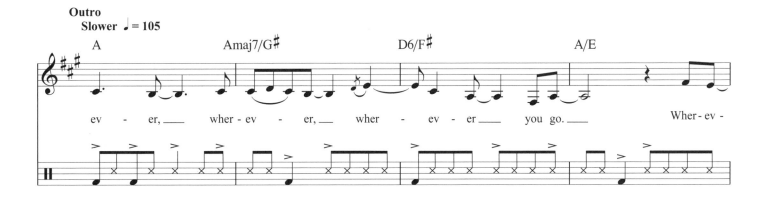

A

Amaj7/G#

D6/F#

A/E

ev - er, _____ wher - ev - er, _____ wher - ev - er _____ you go. _____

Wher - ev -

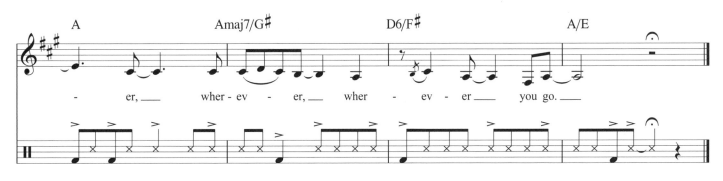

A

Amaj7/G#

D6/F#

A/E

- er, _____ wher - ev - er, _____ wher - ev - er _____ you go. _____

Don't Know Why

Words and Music by Jesse Harris

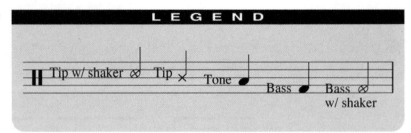

Intro
Moderately slow ♩ = 89

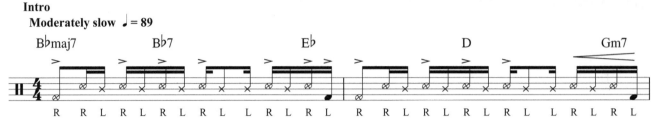

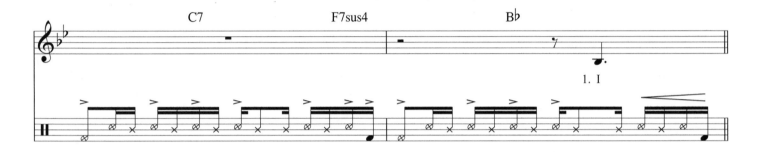

1. I

Verse

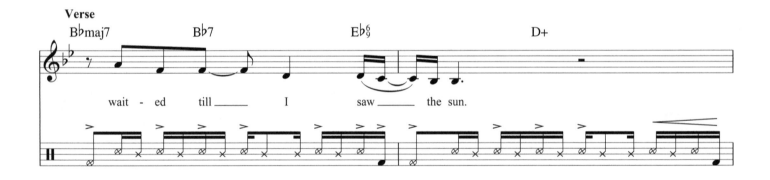

wait - ed till ____ I saw ____ the sun.

I don't know why ____ I did - n't come.

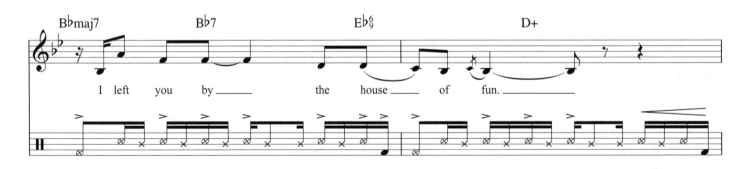

I left you by ____ the house ____ of fun.

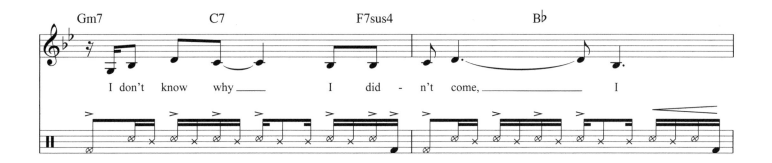

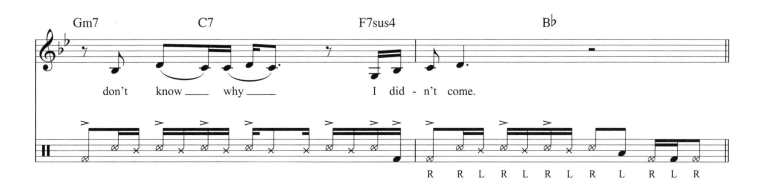

Verse

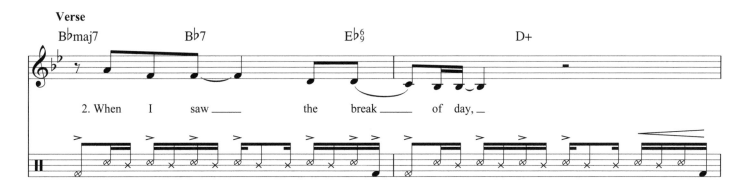

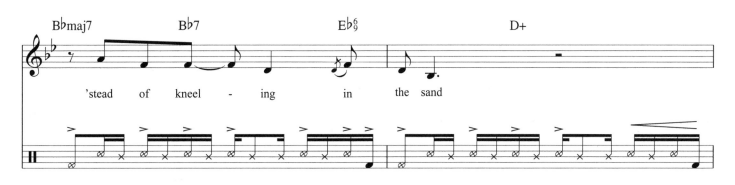

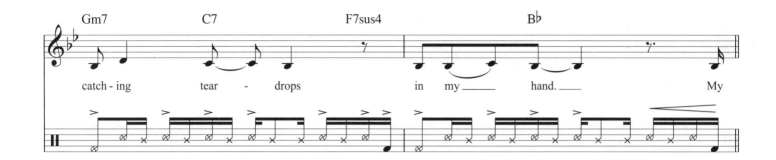

catch - ing   tear - drops   in my ___ hand. ___   My

Bridge

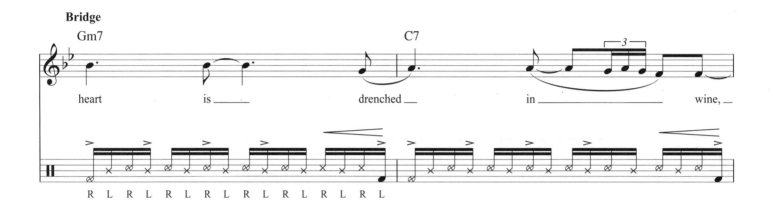

heart   is ___   drenched ___   in _____ wine, ___

R L R L R L R L R L R L R L R L R L

___   yeah, ___   but

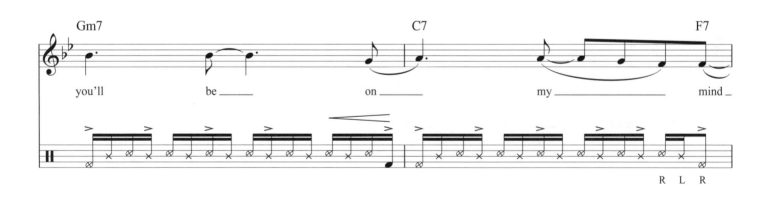

you'll   be ___   on ___   my _____ mind ___

R   L   R

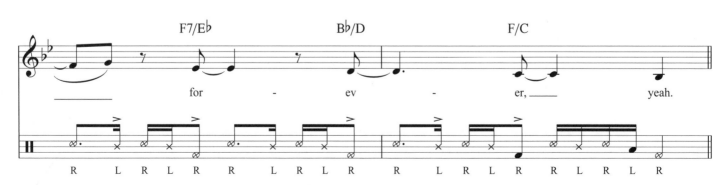

___   for - ev - er, _____   yeah.

R   L   R   L   R   R   L   R   L   R   R   L   R   L   R   R   L   R   L   R

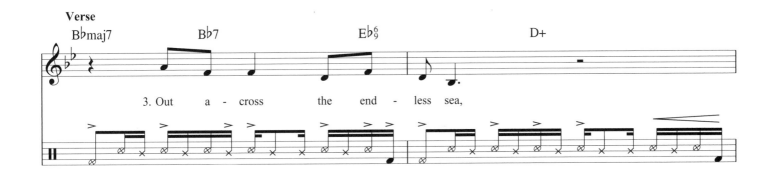

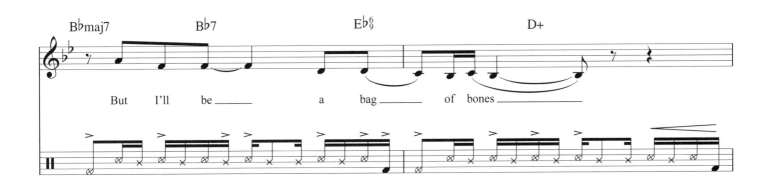

Bridge

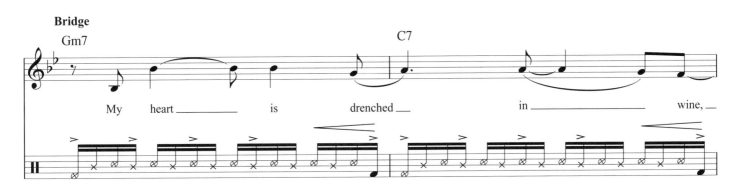

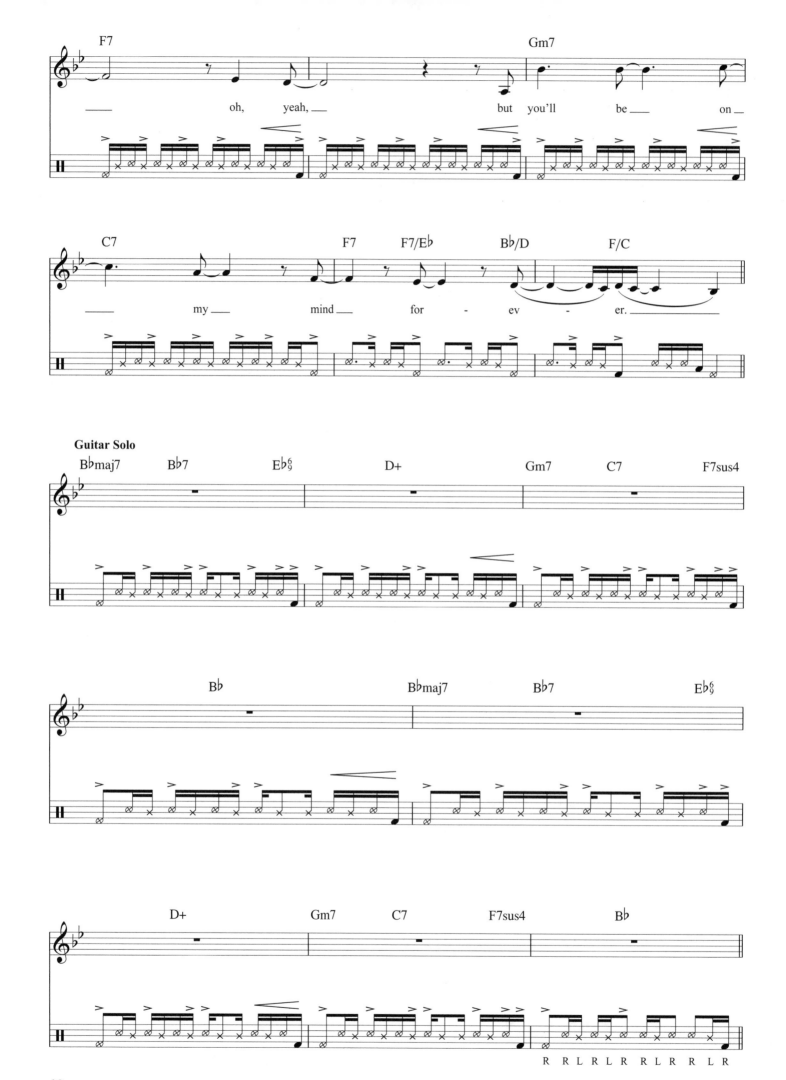

Verse

Mean

Words and Music by Taylor Swift

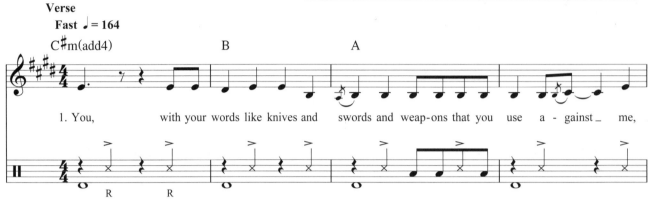

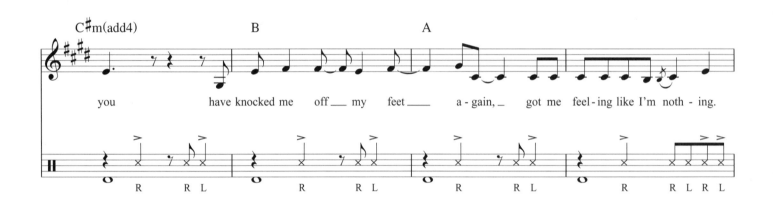

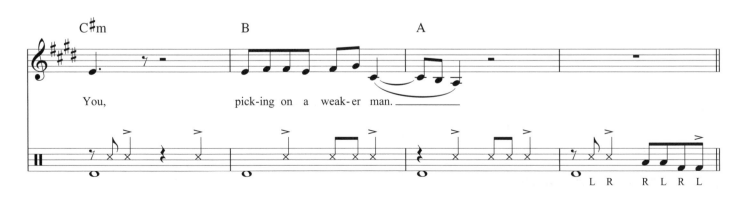

Pre-Chorus

Well, you can take me down _____ with just _ one sin - gle _ blow. _

But you _____ don't know, _ what you _____ don't know. _

Chorus

Some - day, _ I'll be liv - in' in a big ol' cit - y and

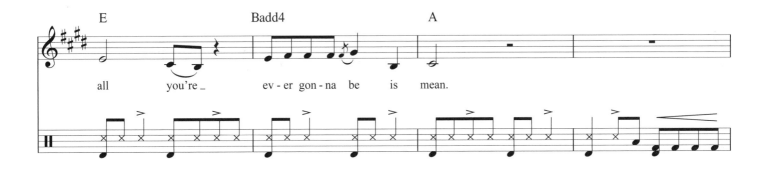

all you're _ ev - er gon - na be is mean.

Some - day, _ I'll be big e - nough so you can't hit me and

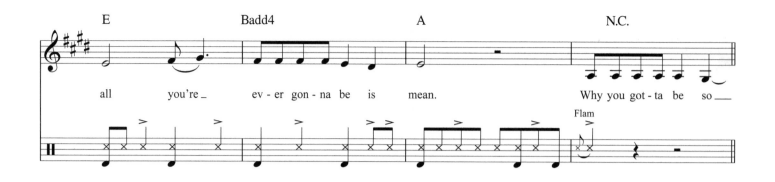

all you're _ ev-er gon-na be is mean. Why you got-ta be so _

Interlude

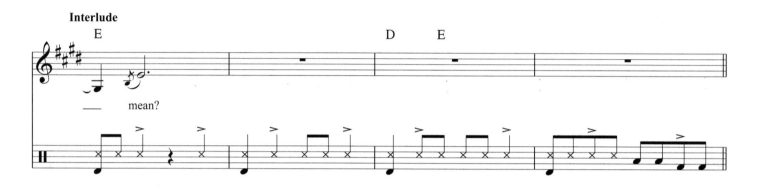

_ mean?

Verse

2. You, with your switch-ing sides and your wild-fire lies and your hu-mil-i-a-tion,

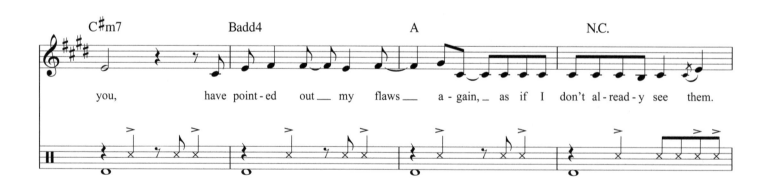

you, have point-ed out _ my flaws _ a-gain,_ as if I don't al-read-y see them.

I walk with my __ head down,_ tryin' to block you out 'cause I'll nev-er im-press you,

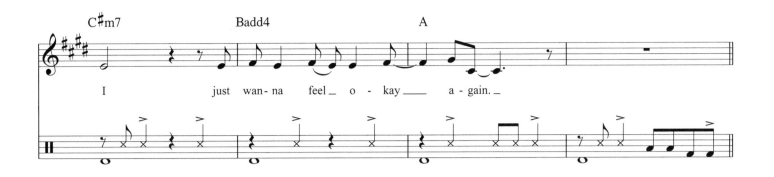

I just wan-na feel __ o-kay __ a-gain. __

Pre-Chorus

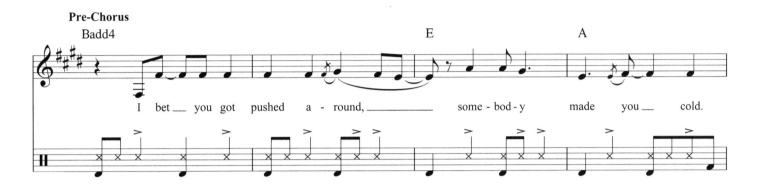

I bet __ you got pushed a-round, ___ some-bod-y made you __ cold.

But the cy-cle ends __ right now, __ 'cause you __ can't lead __ me down __ that road __ and you __

Chorus

__ don't know __ what you __ don't know. __ Some - day, __ I'll be

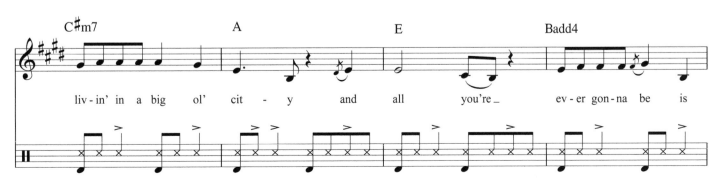

liv-in' in a big ol' cit-y and all you're __ ev-er gon-na be is

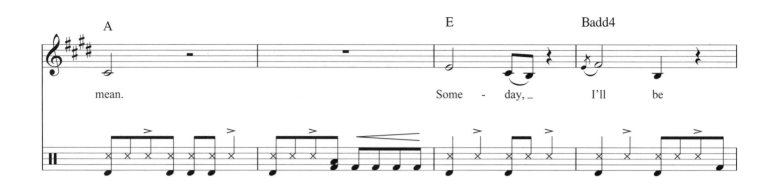

mean.   Some - day, _ I'll be

big e - nough so you can't hit me and all you're _ ev - er gon - na be is

mean.   Why you got - ta be so _____ mean?

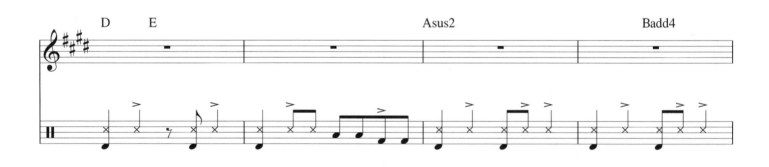

And I can _ see you years _ from now _ in a bar, _

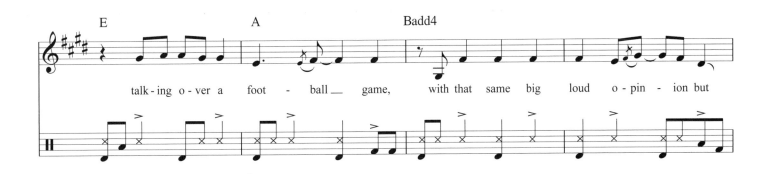

talk-ing o-ver a foot - ball __ game, with that same big loud o-pin - ion but

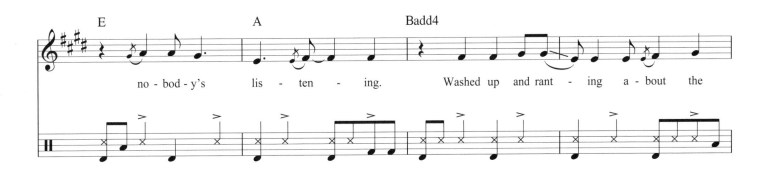

no-bod-y's lis - ten - ing. Washed up and rant - ing a - bout the

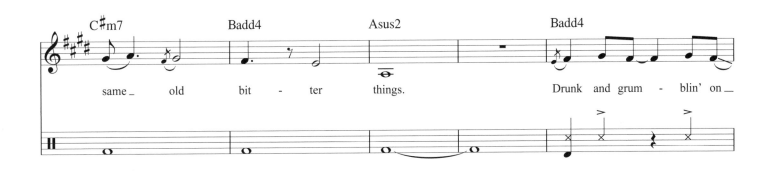

same __ old bit - ter things. Drunk and grum - blin' on __

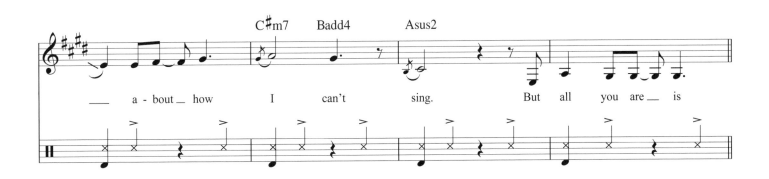

__ a - bout __ how I can't sing. But all you are __ is

Interlude

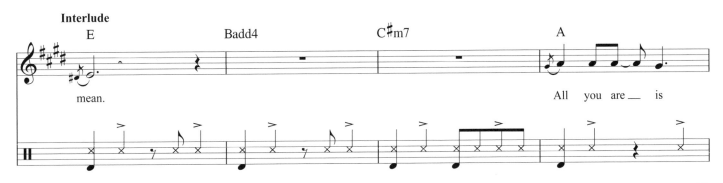

mean. All you are __ is

mean and a li - ar and pa - thet - ic and a - lone in life __ and

mean, and __ mean, and __ mean, and __ mean. But __

Chorus

N.C.

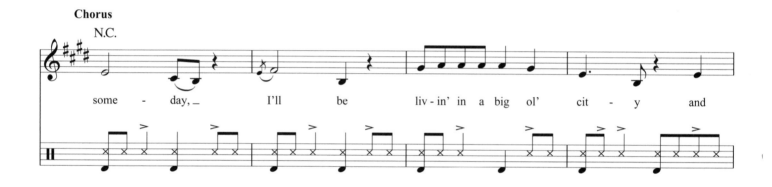

some - day, __ I'll be liv - in' in a big ol' cit - y and

all you're ev - er gon - na be is mean. Yeah! _____

Some - day, __ I'll __ be big e - nough so you can't hit me and

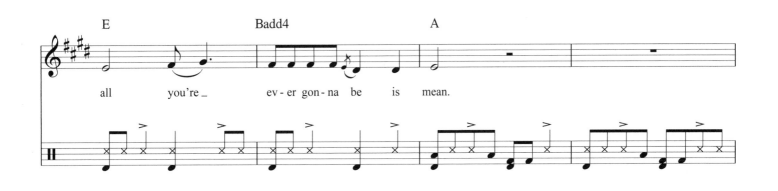

all you're _ ev - er gon - na be is mean.

Some - day, _ I'll be liv - in' in a big ol' cit - y and

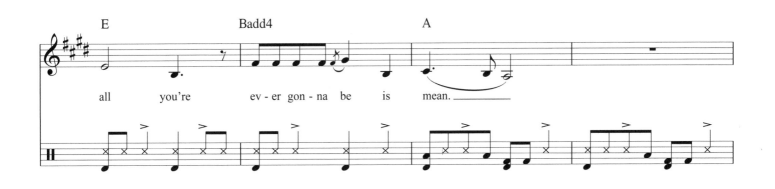

all you're ev - er gon - na be is mean. _____

Some - day, _ I'll _ be big e - nough so you can't hit me and all you're

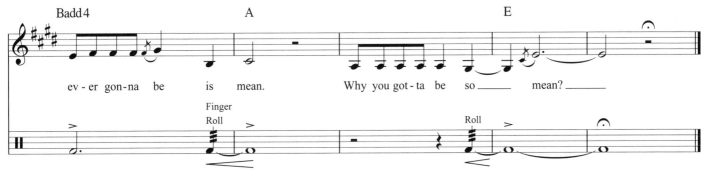

ev - er gon-na be is mean. Why you got - ta be so _____ mean? _____

Fast Car

Words and Music by Tracy Chapman

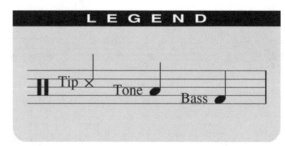

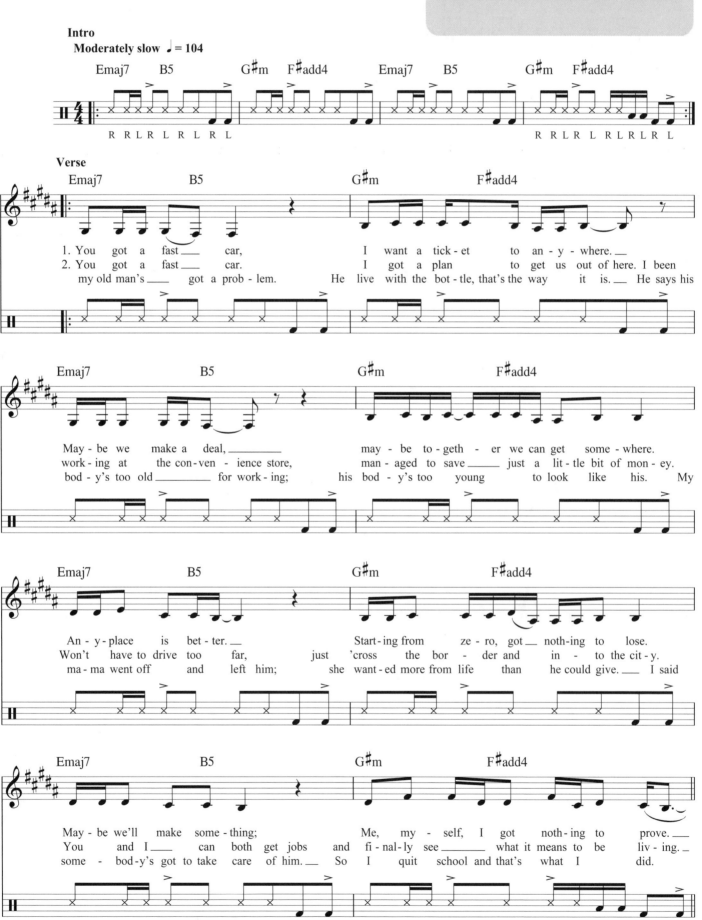

'Cause I re - mem - ber we were

% Chorus

driv - ing, driv - ing in your car, __ the speed so fast __ I felt like __ I was drunk.

Cit - y lights lay out be - fore __ us and your arm felt nice wrapped a - round my shoul - der. And

I, _____ I _____ had a feel - ing that I _____ be - longed. _

R R L R L L L R L R L R R L R L L L R L L

I, _____ I _____ had a feel - ing I _____ could be some - one, _ be some - one, _ be some - one. _

Interlude

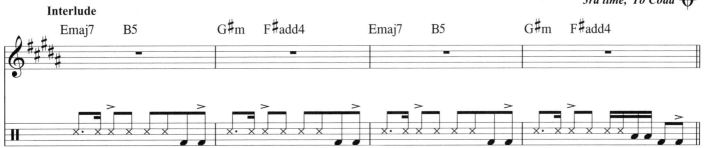

Verse

5. You got a fast ___ car. We go cruis - ing to en - ter - tain our - selves. ___ You
6. You got a fast ___ car. I got a job that pays all our bills. ___ You

still ain't got a job ___ and I work in a mar - ket as a check-out girl. ___
stay out drink - ing late at the bar; see more of your friends than you do of your kids.

I know things ___ will get bet - ter; you'll find work, and I'll ___ get pro - mot - ed. ___
I'd al - ways hoped for bet - ter; thought may - be to - geth-er you and me'd find it.

We'll move out ___ of the shel - ter, buy a big - ger house and live in the sub - urbs. ___
I got no plans, ___ I ain't go - ing no - where, so take your fast car and keep on driv - ing. ___

Strong Enough

Words and Music by Kevin Gilbert, David Baerwald, Sheryl Crow,
Brian McLeod, Bill Bottrell and David Ricketts

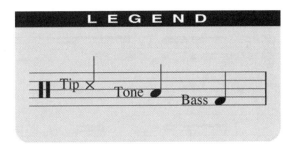

Intro

Moderately slow ♩ = 78

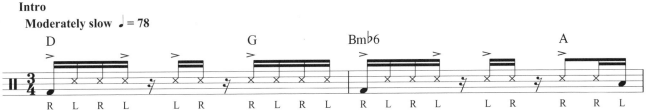

Verse

1. God, I feel ___ like hell ___ to - night. The

tears of rage, ___ I can - not fight. I'd be the

last to help ___ you un - der - stand. Are you

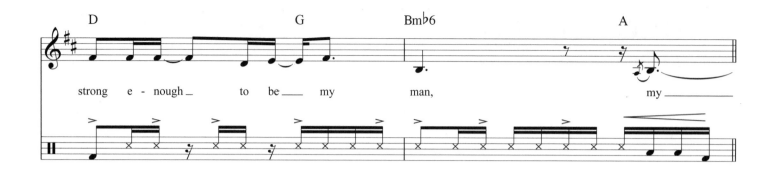

strong e - nough ___ to be ___ my man,   my _____

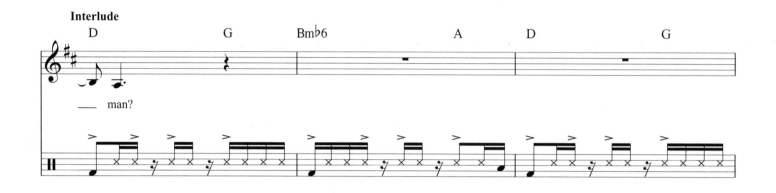

Interlude

___ man?

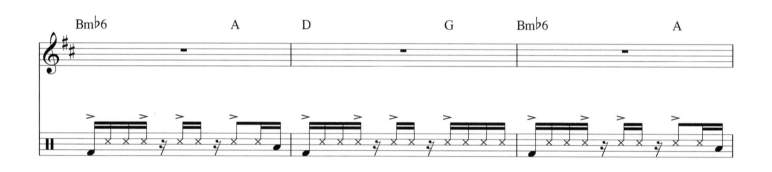

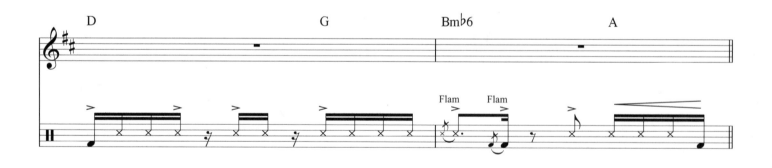

Verse

2. Noth - ing's true ___ when noth - ing's right,   so

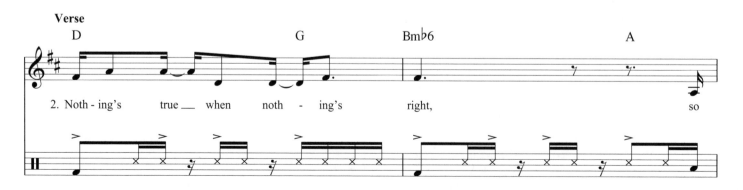

Bridge

Lie _____ to me, _____ but

please don't leave. _____

Interlude

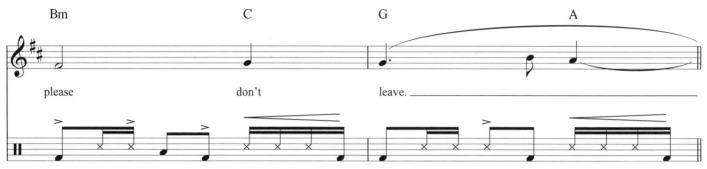

_____ Don't

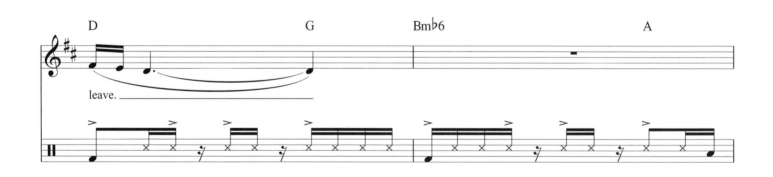

leave. _____

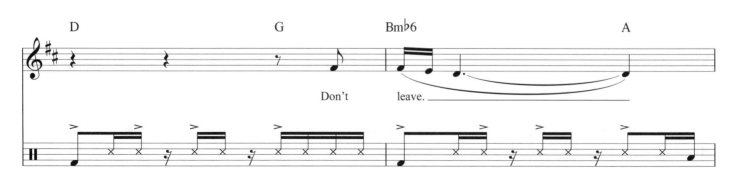

Don't leave. _____

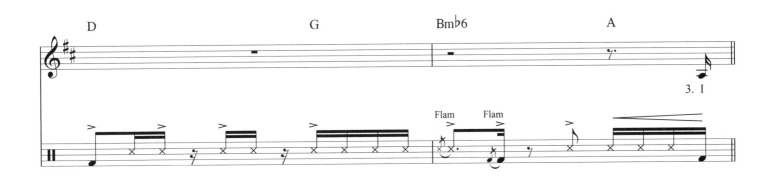

Verse

have a face __ I can - not show,   I

make the rules __ up as __ I go.   Just

try and love __ me if __ you __ can. _____ Are you

strong e - nough __ to be __ my man? _____ My _____

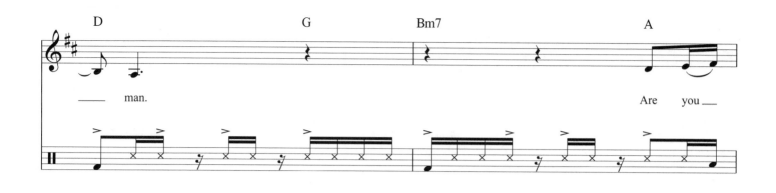

man.   Are you

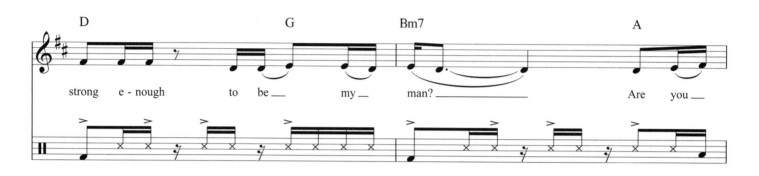

strong e - nough   to   be __   my __   man? _____   Are   you __

strong e - nough   to   be __   my _____   man?   Are   you __

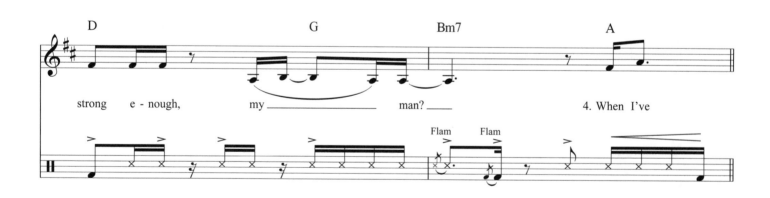

strong e - nough,   my _____ man? ____   4. When I've

Verse

shown you that __ I   just __ don't __   care, _____   when I'm __

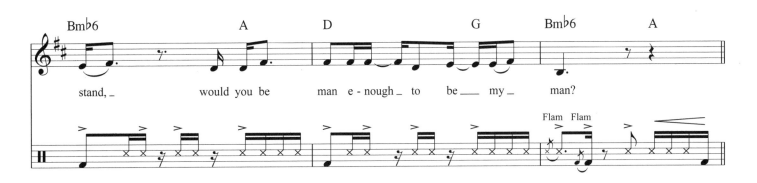

Bridge

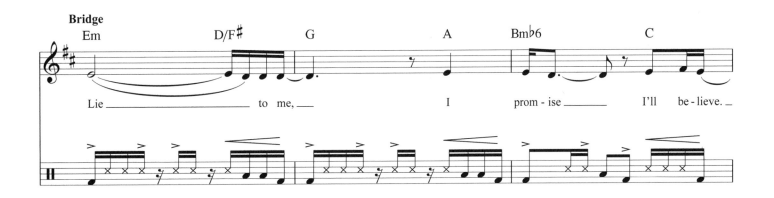

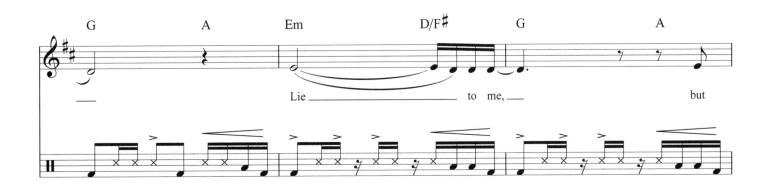

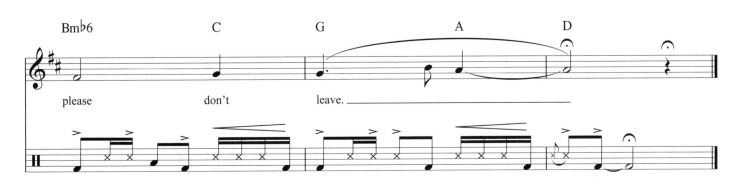

The Way I Am

Words and Music by Ingrid Michaelson

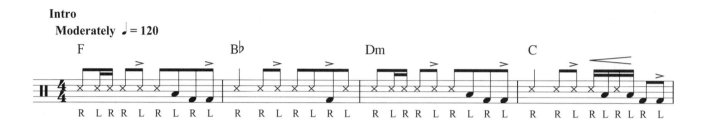

Chorus

I _____ love _____ the way _ you say _ good morn - ing, _____ and

you, _____ you take me the way I _____ am. _____

Verse

2. If you _ are chill - y, here, take my sweat - er. _____

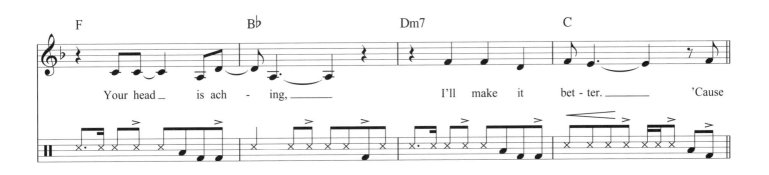

Your head _ is ach - ing, _____ I'll make it bet - ter. _____ 'Cause

Chorus

I _____ love _____ the way _ you call _ me "ba - by," _____ and

you, _____ you, take me the way I am. _____

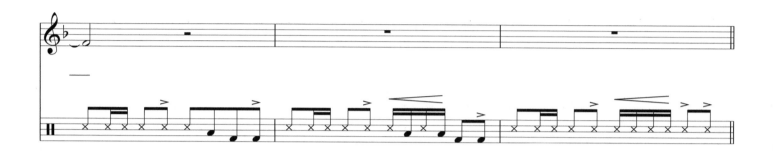

Finger
Roll

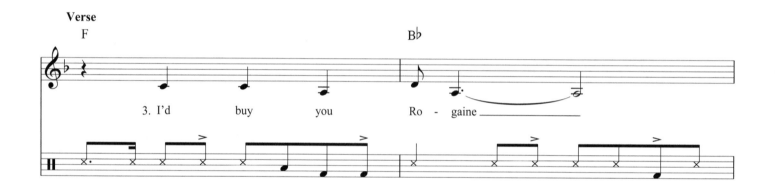

Verse

3. I'd buy you Ro - gaine _____

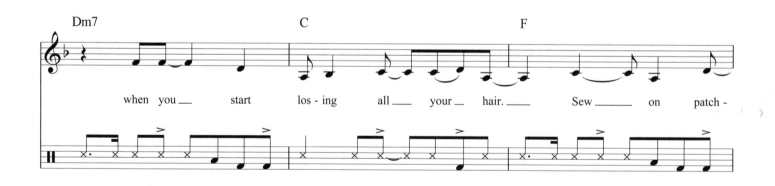

when you ___ start los - ing all ___ your ___ hair. ___ Sew ___ on patch-

- es _____ to all ___ you tear. ___ 'Cause

Chorus

I _____ love _ you more _ than I _____ could ev - er prom-

- ise, _____ and you, _____ you take me the way _ I _____

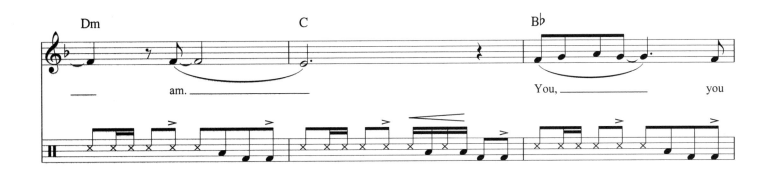

____ am. _____ You, _____ you

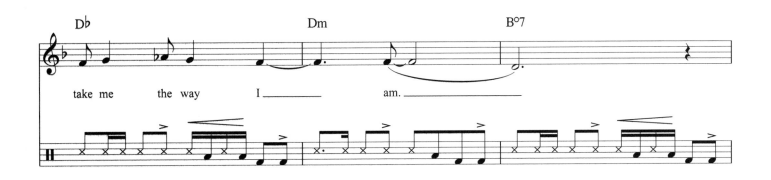

take me the way _ I _____ am. _____

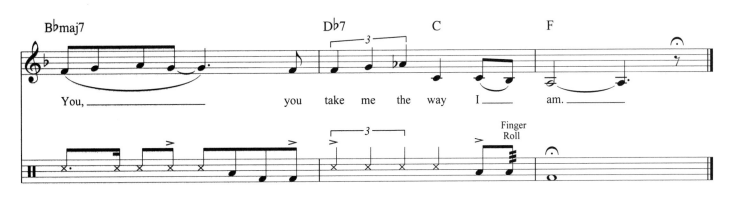

You, _____ you take me the way I _____ am.

Sunny Came Home

Words and Music by Shawn Colvin and John Leventhal

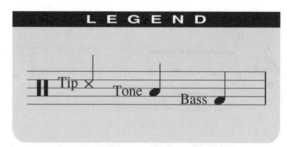

Intro (Lite Cajón)
Moderately slow ♩ = 84

(Full Cajón)

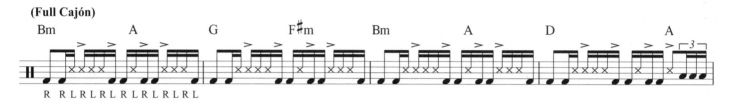

Verse

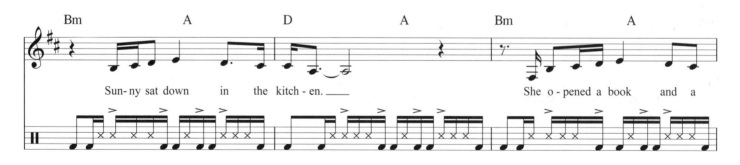

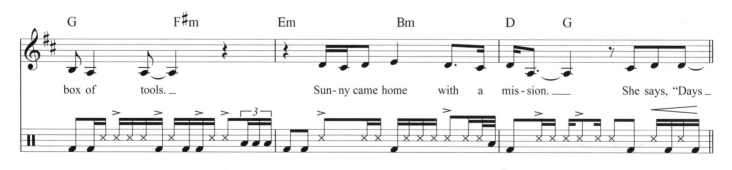

Chorus

go ___ by, ___ I'm ___ hyp - no - tized, ___ I'm walk -

- ing ___ on a ___ wire. ___ I ___ close ___ my ___ eyes ___ and ___ fly

out ___ of ___ my mind ___ in - to the fire." ___

Interlude

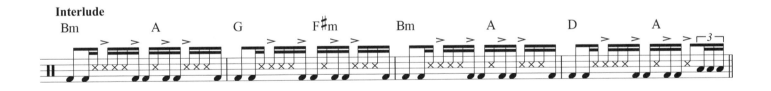

Verse

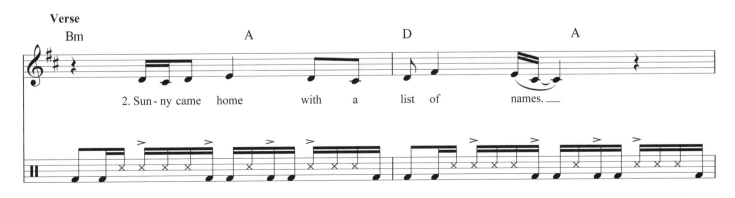

2. Sun - ny came home with a list of names. ___

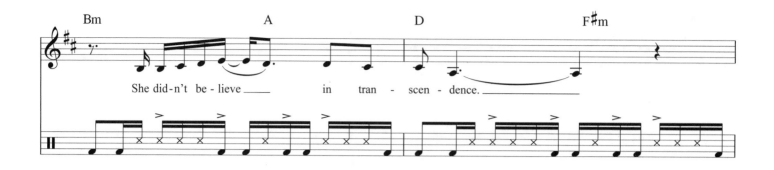

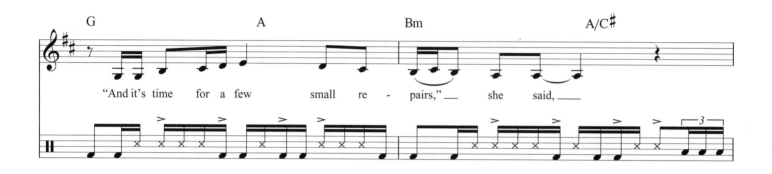

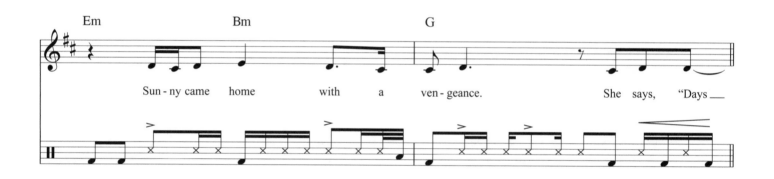

Chorus

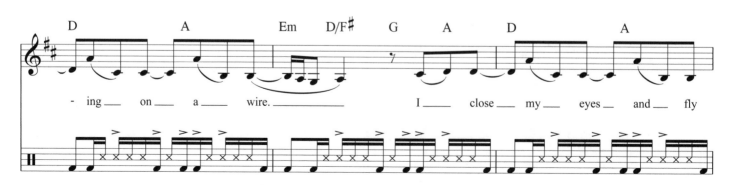

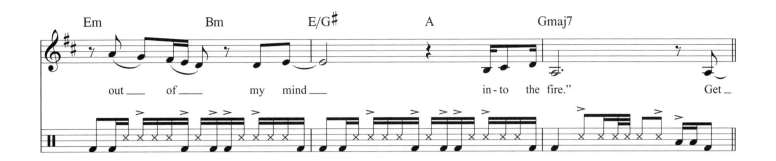

out ___ of ___ my mind ___ in-to the fire." Get ___

Bridge

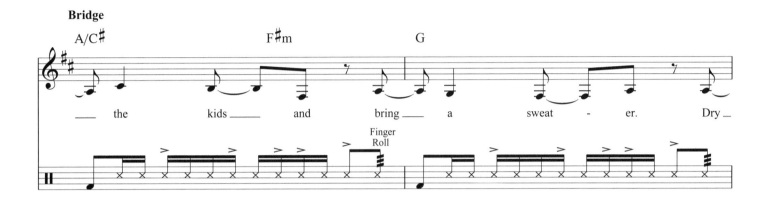

___ the kids ___ and bring ___ a sweat - er. Dry ___

Finger Roll

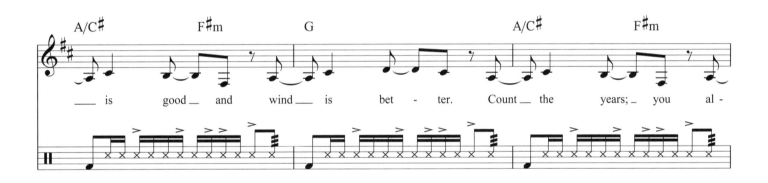

___ is good ___ and wind ___ is bet - ter. Count ___ the years; you al -

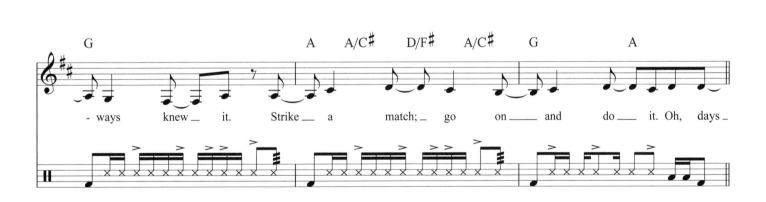

- ways knew ___ it. Strike ___ a match; go on ___ and do ___ it. Oh, days ___

Chorus

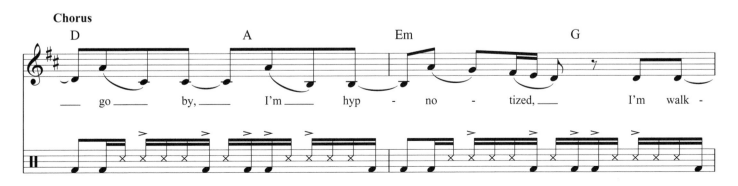

___ go ___ by, ___ I'm ___ hyp - no - tized, ___ I'm walk -

-ing on a wire. I close my eyes and fly

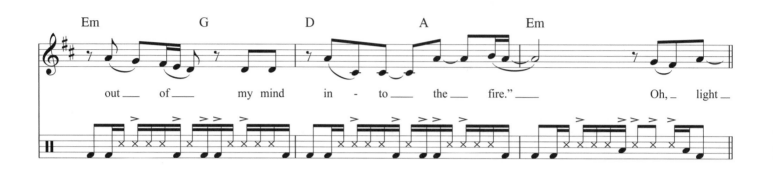

out of my mind in - to the fire." Oh, light

Chorus

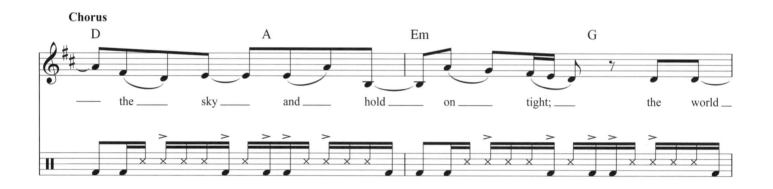

the sky and hold on tight; the world

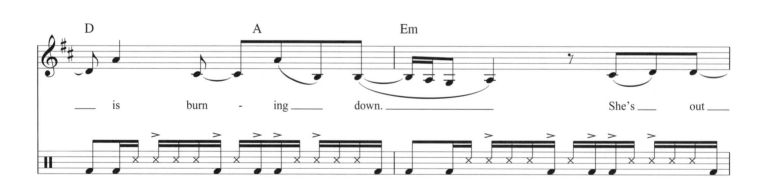

is burn - ing down. She's out

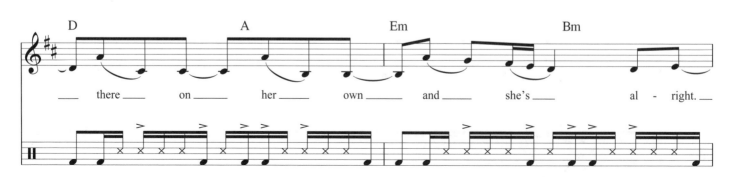

there on her own and she's al - right.

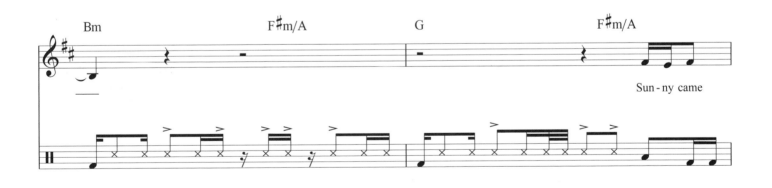

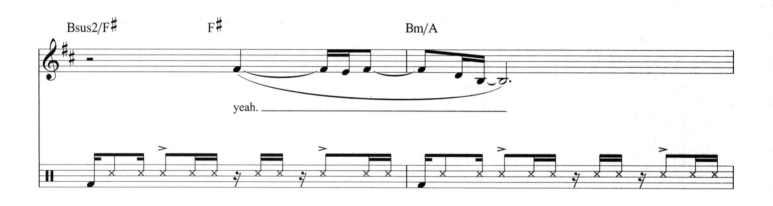

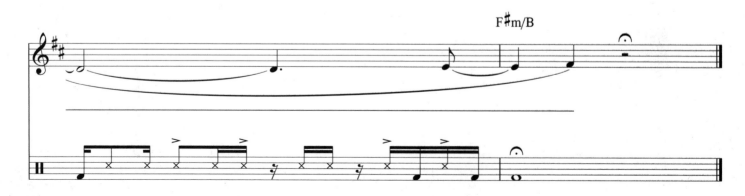